Hermann Warszawiak

"THE LITTLE MESSIANIC PROPHET"

OR

Two Years Labour among the Refugee Jews of New York

With Prefatory Notices by

Rev. ANDREW BONAR, D.D., Glasgow

AND

Rev. J. H. WILSON, D.D., Edinburgh

By C. G. DOUGLAS

WIPF & STOCK · Eugene, Oregon

Wipf and Stock Publishers
199 W 8th Ave, Suite 3
Eugene, OR 97401

Hermann Warszawiak
"The Little Prophet" or Two Years Labour Among
the Refugee Jews of New York
By Douglas, C. G. and Bonar, Andrew
ISBN 13: 978-1-60608-576-9
Publication date 4/30/2010
Previously published by Andrew Elliot, 1892

PREFATORY NOTES.

IT seems to me that what is told in this short narrative of facts is fitted to interest and encourage us in our efforts for the ancient people, more than anything that has taken place since Missions to the Jews began—I might almost say, since Apostolic times. We find here *Jews by hundreds* eagerly listening to the simple story of the Saviour "suffering for sin," the just for the unjust, to bring us unto God. The instrument raised up for the work is an intelligent, lively, single-hearted son of Abraham, born and brought up in Poland, led to Christ in Breslau, and by a series of singular persecutions and dangers sent out to New York, where the Lord had work awaiting him. Warszawiak is thoroughly acquainted with the Bible—Old and New Testaments—and is intensely interested in the conversion of his brethren. He is one that can truly say, "My heart's desire and prayer for Israel is that they may be saved."

He stayed under my roof for some days, and all who met him were deeply impressed with his character—open, natural, kindly; always cheerful and ready to testify from his own experience daily, that the man who has forsaken wife and children, brothers and sister, father and mother, friends and possessions for Christ's sake, receives an hundred-fold even now (Matt. xix. 26) in the joy of his soul.

ANDREW A. BONAR, D.D.,
Glasgow.

THE story of Hermann Warszawiak is one of the deepest interest, as the following pages testify. The way in which he was led to the knowledge and profession of the Christian faith was very remarkable. Happily he was guided, in what seems to have been the great crisis of his life, to one of the ablest and most experienced Jewish missionaries, the Rev. Daniel Edward, of Breslau, whose clear and full evangelical teaching and loving and faithful personal dealing laid a firm foundation for all that has since been. Hermann's address, on the occasion of his baptism, made a profound impression on the many Jews who were present, and was an earnest of the spiritual power which has since so signally marked his preaching and private intercourse with his people. His conversion was his introduction into a new world. He laboured under all the disadvantages of his education and early training as a Jew. He had little human teaching, except that of Mr Edward, during the months of his stay at Breslau; but his constant and prayerful study of God's Word, under the teaching of the Holy Spirit, has wonderfully equipped him as a Christian man and as a teacher of others. When he first came to this country, I lent him a copy which Dr Delitzsch had sent to me of his Hebrew New Testament, and when he returned it he told me that he had read it "hundreds of times," which I can well believe to have been literally true. He seems to realise a living, personal Christ in a very unusual degree. Some of his private letters (all unconsciously on his part) are the nearest approach which I have seen to those of Samuel Rutherford.

The opening to the Jews at New York at present is almost alone of its kind. Instead of solitary inquirers, as in the case of most other Jewish Missions, Mr Warszawiak has had a "wide door and effectual" set before him in public and in private. The finger of God seems to be specially pointing just now in that direction, and it is for the churches and for individual Christians, who have regard to the divine order, "to the Jew first," to be prompt in taking advantage of the great opportunity. It is hoped that the present publication will be a means of calling forth sympathy and prayer and liberal help.

J. H. WILSON.

HERMANN WARSZAWIAK,
"*THE LITTLE MESSIANIC PROPHET;*"
OR
TWO YEARS' LABOUR AMONG THE REFUGEE JEWS OF NEW YORK.

A WONDERFUL sight—one indeed unexampled since the early days of the Christian era—is now to be seen in New York City every Saturday afternoon, viz., a congregation of from three hundred to eight hundred adult Jews, with a small proportion of women, assembled in a Christian church!

And what is the attraction? To hear one of their brethren, quite a young man, prove out of the Scriptures that Jesus is the Christ, and testify, from a full and loving heart, that He, Jesus, their brother, the Son of David, the Son of God, is able to save to the uttermost all who come unto God by Him.

Had these crowds gathered for a few weeks only, moved by curiosity to see and hear the grandson of a well-known and much-venerated rabbi, or to engage in those keen discussions in which learned Jews delight, and produce a scene of angry disputation and violence, this would have been nothing unusual; but the remarkable fact is that these Saturday gatherings—begun in April 1890 with a meeting numbering sixteen men—have steadily increased in numbers till now, in January 1892, the church, schoolroom, and adjacent class-rooms of 280 Rivington Street, will not contain the numbers that seek to obtain admission; and whereas there was at the outset restlessness and strong efforts to disturb the meetings and break them up, the majority now determinedly range themselves on the side of the preacher, and do not allow their own enjoyment of the sermon to be interfered with.

The *New York Observer* of October 17, 1891, has an article, entitled "A Wonderful Work." From it we quote the following sentences:—" On a recent Saturday, when we attended this service, every seat was occupied. Only men occupied the ground floor, and nearly all of these were comparatively young. All were decently clad, and had the appearance of being in comfortable circumstances. Their attention to the discourse of the missionary, Mr Warszawiak, was remarkable for its intelligent and decorous recognition of the points made by the speaker. He speaks in a foreign tongue with intense earnestness, graphic power, effective action, all his faculties and powers of mind and body being successfully engaged in his evangelistic work. It would be impossible not to hear and be interested in his message. But of course *the wonder is, that this inaccessible class of people will come, week after week, to the number of five and six and seven hundred at a single service.*"

The Rev. A. L. Love of St Louis writes on the same subject a few weeks later:—" The Saturday I visited the work, over six hundred men filled all available space long before the hour for the sermon. The police had refused further admission, and a throng of about as many more disappointed men filled the street. When I reached the building, the doors were again closed, and a like throng was without, blocking the way. They were gathered in groups, intently discussing the claims to Messiahship of this Jesus, and the utterances of the eloquent speaker within. I was forced to seek a private entrance. The librarian, in an adjoining building, kindly took me down through two cellars and up a narrow stairway, and thrust me through a door in the rear of the room. What a sight! The audience was no longer orderly seated, but every one, rising to his feet, had pressed forward to the edge of the platform, and there, in densest crowd, the six or seven hundred listened, some with angry faces and fierce mutterings, some with clenched fists shaken at the speaker, but every word was eagerly caught. There was no mistaking the nationality of the audience, or of the preacher for that matter. They were Jews beyond question, and as any Hebrew merchant anxious to 'sell you dat coad, sheap,' so the preacher, with elevated shoulders, outstretched hands and inclined head, was persuading them to accept their own Messiah. Mr Warszawiak cannot yet be thirty, but he is a man of tremendous power and intensity. At the close of the service it was a wonder to see with what power he could control the angry opposers with a few words here and there, passing fearlessly through the crowd so dense that an officer had to make way for him. Two or three hundred copies of the New Testament in Hebrew were gratuitously given those who went to the platform, also tracts in German, but the supply was exhausted before half the jostling, anxious seekers were supplied. Half an hour after, though besought to go home, a hundred or more, determined to see and hear everything, would not comply till after the preacher had left the room. It is a glorious work, with largest promise of rapid and far-reaching extension."

The question has often been asked by persons who have heard of this remarkable movement among the Jews of New York, Who is the missionary that has such power over his people, and of what society is he the agent? It is the object of this little booklet to answer these questions, so that glory may be given to Him who chose and prepared an instrument fitted for His work, and thrust him out into the field which He Himself had plowed up and prepared to receive the seed of the Kingdom.

A baby boy was born in Warsaw in March 1865 in a Jewish home. He was one of a large family, his parents devout and strictly orthodox, his mother of the well-known Rabbinical family of Gura—which is the head of the Jews of Eastern Europe. From earliest childhood, Hermann was taught the sacred language, and trained to walk in all the commandments and ordinances of the law blameless. Favoured boy, born of a favoured race, having the knowledge of the one true God, one of the peculiar people, of the innermost circle of Israel—what more could he desire? But painfully as he observed the six hundred and thirteen precepts of Moses—and the thousands of precepts of the Talmud, fasted, prayed and did penance, his conscience still knew no rest; and the words addressed to him by his uncle, the Chief Rabbi, under whose roof he had the privilege of living after he became a "son of the law," "Prepare to meet thy God," never left him. He tried to become as holy as his venerated uncle, who is by inheritance the head of the Chassidim, thinking thus to be fully prepared to meet God; but still the sense of sin and unworthiness pursued him. His childhood and youth were full of sadness; with delicate health, an earnest, sensitive, devout nature, and an awakened conscience, he had no rest—he felt the need of atonement, and sin-offering there was none. On this point he said himself, in his baptismal address, "No one who knows my family history can doubt that I was brought up piously, and I cast in my lot heart and soul with the Chassidim, studied diligently the Talmud and the Holy Scriptures, for I wanted to become righteous and holy, but the transgression of the law brought me to the knowledge that I was only a lost sinner, as every day in one way or other I transgressed the law. For though the five books of Moses only contain six hundred and thirteen precepts, yet the Talmud, which the Jews, and especially the Chassidim, accept equally, has multiplied the number of precepts which must be obeyed. It is impossible to observe even the six hundred and thirteen commands; and Moses says, 'Cursed is every one that continueth not in all things that are written in the book of the law to do them.'"

After the custom of his people, he was betrothed in his fourteenth year to the daughter of a rich Jewish banker and merchant at Lodz, Poland, and two years later this young couple were married and took up their abode with the wife's parents. The young son-in-law was treated with much respect and consideration because of his priestly and rabbinical descent, and lived in the enjoyment of every luxury. He pursued his studies with a view to following the example of two elder brothers, who are rabbis in Polish cities, and having great gifts of eloquence, he frequently preached in the synagogue at Lodz, attracting such crowds as to excite the jealousy of the stated rabbi. But from the study of the law, the young preacher went on to read and examine fully the books of the Prophets, and there he got glimpses of salvation for Israel and relief for his own burdened conscience, in Him whom Isaiah sets forth as wounded for our transgressions, bruised for our iniquities, healing us with His stripes; and in that new covenant that Jeremiah proclaims in all its glory. These, then, were the favourite themes of the young rabbi. His sermons created deep interest, but also anger and alarm. The finger of scorn was pointed at him as an apostate, and his own parents and those of his wife agreed that he should no longer remain at Lodz, but return to Warsaw, leaving his wife and two little children behind in the meantime. They had no doubt that under his father's roof, and fully engaged in mercantile affairs, he would soon be cured of his mad folly. But the Good Shepherd had His eye all the while on the poor lost sheep. We need not follow all his wanderings, but hurry on to the happy day when Jesus found him; old things passed away, and all henceforth became new. In July 1889, the subject of this sketch found himself in Breslau. His mind was restless and disturbed, and walking down the public promenade on the Lord's day, his ear was attracted by the sound of singing, and his eye by a placard announcing what proved to be the sermon of the Rev. Daniel Edward, the venerable Scotch missionary to the Jews. Hermann entered, stood near the door—and was thrilled by the heartfelt prayer to which he listened, and the sermon on John x. 16, 17. After the sermon he asked a young man standing near if he could give him the address of the preacher. "Oh, yes, that I can—but come and speak to him now," and so ere ever he was aware, he found himself taken to the heart of one of Christ's servants, by whom all the day long He stretched out His hands to a disobedient and gainsaying people. Mr Edward and Hermann Warszawiak sat down at once, Scripture in hand, and for three hours were unconscious of the lapse of time, while the aged teacher answered the questions of the anxious inquirer. At that time Hermann Warszawiak had no intention whatever of becoming a Christian. He would be the last man to bring sorrow and disgrace on his loved mother, and on his large and honoured family connection, but an insatiable desire to know the truth possessed him. Though he knew it not, it was Jesus Himself who followed after him, and so every passage of Scripture that Mr Edward quoted did its work; he could not refrain from hearing more; he vowed never to speak again to the missionary, but could not keep his word. For three months the daily earnest searching into the Scriptures, and comparing of New Testament with Old, went on, the instruction being all conveyed in the Hebrew tongue, which gave it tenfold force to this son of Israel. As one grand truth after another evolved itself, he got into amazement, exclaiming, "I am sure if these things could be spoken in Warsaw, not hundreds, but thousands would soon turn to the Lord." The life of Him, who is holy, harmless, undefiled and separate from sinners, who is all love, and who spake the words of the Sermon on the Mount, deeply impressed the young man, by its contrast to the orthodox piety of Judaism, which has no such high standard of truth and goodness. Mr Edward refused to leave Breslau or take any summer rest, lest any interruption of these momentous lessons should have serious consequences; and at the end of that time, not only was the mind of the inquirer satisfied, but his heart was won for the Lord Jesus Christ —the way unto the Father, in whom at last he had found peace with God. Then came a terrible struggle.

Must father and mother, brothers and sister, property, good name, yea even wife and little children, be forsaken, to win Christ and be found in Him? His physical strength was quite prostrated; he lay on a sick bed, and thought himself nigh unto death; but in that solemn hour, Christ won the victory, and he said to his friend and teacher, "Now I am ready: baptize me to-morrow if you will." Accordingly on the 6th October 1889, Hermann Warszawiak was baptized by the Rev. D. Edward in the presence of the ordinary congregation, a considerable number of Jews and Jewesses being present. He gave a powerful address before baptism in the German language, which has been published.

Mr Edward was deeply impressed, while studying the Scriptures with Hermann Warszawiak, that here was a man called of God, not only for his own soul's sake, but for his brethren, and he hoped to retain him in Germany to be his fellow-worker among the people of Israel; but in a few days the news of the baptism at Breslau spread to Poland; his relatives were rich, and determined they would leave nothing undone to get the young man into their power: there was nothing for it but immediate flight. Mr Edward hurried him off to Scotland, commending him to the kindness of the Jewish Committee of the Free Church, and of two or three private friends. The first joy of deliverance from sin, and assured salvation in Christ, was upon the young disciple when he landed in Edinburgh, still he was all bleeding and torn with the struggle that had broken every earthly tie, and the six months spent in Edinburgh in great seclusion, lest his enemies should discover where he was, were also months of much suffering and crying unto God—"sorrowful, yet alway rejoicing," "persecuted, but not forsaken; cast down, but not destroyed." During these six months he learnt much through secret prayer, study of the word, and the ministry of the Rev. Dr J. H. Wilson; he won life-long Christian friends, and had just acquired enough English to profit by attendance on classes in the New College, with a view to being ordained as a missionary to the Jews, when again the summons came, "Arise, and go hence," and within three days the home in Edinburgh, plans for the future, and sympathetic friends, were all left behind, and the subject of our narrative is crossing the ocean to America.

This sudden and seemingly sad change, was outwardly caused by the fact that his persecutors had tracked him out, and the Scotch friends said, "We can no longer protect you: all we can do for you is to send you to America." But now, after the event, it is clear that the Lord was thrusting him out for immediate work, that having heard the Saviour's voice, he might at once say to his brethren, "Come," and an inward sense that he *was* sent of God, upheld him. It was indeed a dreary, terrible moment when the poor fugitive—alone, almost penniless, with no friends to receive him on the other shore, and no prospect in life—started on his journey, and one among the company, who escorted him to the train, uttered in three short words "Er geht mit" (He goes with), the only consolation that was possible. It was enough. He went in the strength of that word, and has lived till now on this experience, "Lo, I am with you alway." "He that forsaketh not *all* that he hath, cannot be my disciple," are our Lord's emphatic words, but Christians born and bred are seldom put to this test. Warszawiak counted the price not too high when at his baptism he bargained for precious Jesus Christ, the anointed Saviour; but there lingered in his heart the hope that his own flesh and blood, his wife and little girls, might be spared to him, and become fellow-heirs with himself of the grace of life. He often said to friends in Edinburgh, "There are three souls that I am bound to save before I can go forth as a missionary to others," and there was for a time great reason to hope that this desire of his heart was to be immediately granted. But it pleased the Lord further to prove His servant. He said in unmistakable providences, "Wait for no one, for nothing, go forth *at once*, and be my witness to your brethren of the lost sheep of the house of Israel now scattered abroad." He obeyed, and has reaped the reward in an inward peace and strength till then unknown, and in the marked and special blessing that from the first attended his labours.

Finding himself for the first time quite alone on board the Atlantic steamer (for with true Christian kindness the Rev. J. G. Cunningham had accompanied him to Liverpool, and strengthened his hands in God), Satan came to him, tempting him, and said, "You flatter yourself that you are sent by Jehovah to carry the message of salvation to your brethren in America; but how do you know that God sends you? You are flying from your persecutors in Europe: if you stand up in New York and preach Christ, your brethren, far from listening to you, will set on you and kill you at once." But He that is with us is stronger than all they that can be against us. Warszawiak's thoughts reverted to Jonah. He took up that book, and read till he came to chap. iii. 2, "Arise, go unto Nineveh, that great city, and preach unto it the preaching that I bid thee." Here was his commission. The task appointed was not more impossible than that assigned to Jonah, one weak man, the voice of the Lord to great and mighty Nineveh. He went forward with fresh courage and simply obedient, landed on a Friday, 28th March 1890, in New York, and the next day preached Christ to a little company of sixteen adult Jews, who said, "These are good words, we never heard them before," and readily promised to come again the next Sabbath (Saturday) and bring others with them.

Having given this outline of the history of him who soon acquired the name among his brethren in New York of "The Little Messianic Prophet," it will be better to let him tell the narrative of the Lord's work committed to him in that city in his own words, by means of copious extracts from letters, originally written in German, and addressed to a Scotch friend, who stands to him in the relation of a Christian mother. These letters are not reports, were often written in great haste during moments snatched from sleep, but all the more they present to the reader the man as he is, and the work as it developed week by week.

Truth to say, Warszawiak's mission-work commenced on board the *Teutonic*. He found willing hearers among his Jewish fellow-passengers, and distributed to them New Testaments and Gospels. While waiting on the Lord to open up his field of labour, he lost no time in making Jewish acquaintances, preached two or three times in Mr Freshman's Hebrew Christian church, delivered his letters of introduction, and through the influence of Rev. Dr Hall, first got the use of a hall in one of the churches of the City Mission, the "De Witt Memorial," and was afterwards engaged as city missionary for the district surrounding that church. Thousands of Jews had within two or three years come from Russia, Poland, and Germany, and filled the tenement houses in that part of the city; it was fast becoming a Jewish quarter, and the City Mission were glad to secure the services of a man so able to cope with the difficulty of how to reach the heart and mind of this peculiar people.

While still waiting for a definite field of labour, Mr Warszawiak wrote to his friend in Edinburgh:—

New York, April 15, 1890.—Already I find much mission work to do among the Jews here, and yet my heart is much in Scotland. You know it cost me much blood and great conflict till I could consider Jesus Christ as my very own, till I could resolve to give up all, all; yes, all and everything, so as to possess Him. But since then I find that I have lost *nothing*, for what I have found is a million times more valuable than what I, so to speak, have given up. What can be more valuable to me than my salvation, and that through a Son of God, through *the* Son of God, who gave up more, certainly much more, and came down from heaven to deliver me from all evil and all sin, and has given me eternal life? This precious conviction more than makes up to me for all losses, etc. And now I have received still more grace from the dear Son of God, for He is come nearer and nearer to me, and has revealed that He has indeed taken up his abode in my heart (for which I must thank Him to all eternity). . . . Now from yesterday—

I have got the use of the large De Witt Memorial Buildings in which to carry on my work.

April 22, 1890.—You will see from my last letter that I am *firmly* resolved, more and more, to give myself up entirely to my dear Saviour, and to leave everything in His hands, calling on Him daily. And now since I made this firm resolution, the dear faithful Lord and Saviour has come much nearer to me, and His Holy Spirit says within me, "Fear nothing, I go with thee, and will make thee a living witness to my people Israel. Stand up and proclaim My name with all *zeal* and power; fear not, I, Jesus, protect thee, and *go with thee.*" Yes, truly, the Lord spoke thus to me by His Holy Spirit. I used to say, "Do I not deceive myself? Is it possible that God should thus dwell with man?" But now I see clearly what is expected of me in heaven. Why have I been so specially tried? Why have I been driven from place to place? Why have I been torn away from my loved ones? Why have I been separated even from my dear Christian friends, and sent so far, far away? It is all from Him, all from Him, and it is all right. I have now taken His last command specially to heart, and proclaim His Name every day with the greatest zeal, and stand amid Judaism as a living witness. My work is now begun in the De Witt Memorial Church. Last Sabbath (Saturday) a great number of Jews were present at my service. I thank God for all, but specially that He strengthens me by His Holy Spirit, and is come so near to strengthen me,

April 28.—I have just come home from our meeting full of joy. There were only sixteen Jews present, but all so earnest and sincere. It was glorious to see the seriousness depicted on every face, and it was so quiet, so still, when I was speaking about the truth of Christ. I spoke on Isaiah lv. 1-5. My text was the 3d verse, "Hear, and your soul shall live." When I invited them to return the following Sabbath, they all answered, "Oh, yes; with the greatest of pleasure, we will come." Ah, how I thank the dear Lord who gives me new strength, and has opened such a wonderful door for His people.

May 12.—I went with a sore and heavy heart to my meeting to-day, but I cannot describe to you what a glorious meeting it was. When I got there, I found the room completely filled with Jews, and the Rev. Mr Elsing (English pastor of De Witt Church) found it necessary to announce that the following Sabbath (D.V.) we should meet in the church itself. I spoke on Zech. viii. 7, and the Lord seemed to open many hearts to receive the truth that Jesus is the only Saviour. More than sixty adult Jews went away with their countenances shining with joy, in the hope that they had found the promised Messiah. Also yesterday, at a quarter past four, a great many of these Jews came to the German service, longing to hear the praises of Jesus Christ. In truth, there is a great awakening of the New York Jews, and a fourth part of those who attend my meeting are of my uncle's "Chassidim," and knew me formerly. Whatever comes of it, I praise and thank

God in Christ for His wonderful leadings, and am resolved to await them quietly. Should my father or father-in-law come here in search of me, the dear Lord will certainly protect me.

May 24.—I thank the dear Lord and Saviour for the glorious door He has opened for my dear outcast people. Our meeting to-day was more glorious than ever, and the interest that the Jews take is to be seen in the regularity with which they attend every meeting. The Rev. Mr Elsing said he had counted 113 Jews in the meeting, of whom seventy have been regular attendants. I preached to-day, by the request of many Jews, on the Trinity in unity of God. The texts were, Isaiah xlviii. 16, lxiii. 3-9; Deut. vi. 4; Mal. i. 6, etc. Thanks be to God I succeeded in convincing many of the Jews present that the Father and the Son and the Holy Ghost are one God. I made use also of many passages out of the books of "Sohas" and "Talkot" [Jewish Dogmatics]. What makes me most thankful is, that the seed I sow falls on prepared ground. Two very earnest Jews, Mr Besterman, from Cracow, and Mr Perlmutter, from Warsaw, have already applied for baptism. The latter is one of the "Chassidim," and a very learned, upright Jew. I give them daily instruction, and hope that they will become very pious Christians. Amen. As to myself, I can only say that I work to my uttermost, and every meeting leaves me thoroughly exhausted. As you know, after every sermon I conduct a free discussion, which is more fatiguing than to preach for ten hours; but I know for whom I work. He who has given me eternal life is worthy of much more, and I will work on till the hour when He takes me to Himself.

July 4.—I have much to tell you to-day. Our friend from Warsaw, Mr Perlmutter, is now become a brother in the Lord Jesus Christ. He has been baptized, and believes that he has found salvation in Christ. For different reasons, the baptism did not take place with us in the De Witt Church, but in the 9th Street. The Rev. Mr Zemberlin baptized him. All the same, praise be given to our dear Lord, who has received him. May He keep him faithful to the great day! Amen. It is also to be hoped that Mr Besterman will soon be also joined to the Lord. But there is a dear, good man, Jacob See, and Israel Rosenblatt, of whom I must tell you. The first is of German birth, and ever since I came here has regularly attended my meetings. Yet he seldom spoke a word—he is a very quiet man—specially earnest, and has now a very powerful love in his heart to Jesus, and wishes much to belong to Him. As he now tells me, he has paid the greatest attention to all my addresses, and has studied everything carefully afterwards at home, and he has now, also, acquired considerable knowledge of the New Testament. He has learnt by heart the "Lord's Prayer," and "God is Love," etc., and entreated me to baptize him. It is wonderful how this Jew has been laid hold of by Jesus. He will lead him further. The second, Mr Rosenblatt, is from Russia—a very learned Jew, who every Sabbath disputed with us most violently, and maintained that we spoke only falsehoods. This man is now overcome by the word of the Gospel, and he acknowledged at our last meeting, in the presence of many Jews, that Jesus is the Christ, and the New Testament true.

July 7.—If it was not so very hot to-day, I should have more strength, and would be able to write you all particulars of our last meeting. It was very largely attended. After my sermon a little panic occurred during the hours of debate, because several Jews—new-comers—did not believe our affirmation that Jesus Christ is the Saviour of the world and the Lord of the Sabbath. Then Mr Rosenblatt stood up, and spoke for about ten minutes, bearing witness for Jesus. All the Jews were silent with astonishment, as they all know what a learned man he is, and that he was the bitterest enemy of Jesus till quite recently. They expected him to speak on their side. He concluded his address with the following words in the Russian language:—" My beloved, what is the use of fighting? for I am convinced we fight against the Most High, Jesus the Crucified, who in truth accomplished the greatest deed ever done upon earth. Let us rather confess that our forefathers acted very wickedly, and look up to God, to Him whom we have smitten, and in whom to-day we may find forgiveness. He is pure love and mercy. Do you wonder at me? I can only say the Torah (Bible) has convinced me, and if you seek as earnestly as I have done, you will surely find." Then dear Jacob See added a few words with tears. For the third time I am interrupted in writing by the heat, the fiery heat which every five minutes fairly knocks me down. It is really unbearable, and gives one at times such headaches that everything swims before one's eyes.

August 29, 1890.—How can I tell you how gloriously the Lord worked last night at the Rev. Mr Elsing's English service, at which I also gave an address, and some Jews were present. After I had spoken, Mr Elsing opened the meeting for testimony, and several men and women bore witness for Jesus our Lord. Then Mr Elsing asked the Jews present if any of them had anything to say, offering to translate for them into English. After a long silence a Jew stood up and said with deep seriousness, "I am ashamed to confess that I have not found Jesus, but He has found me. Three months ago I went past this church one Sabbath, and seeing many Jews go in, I went in too. Horror seized me when I heard the sermon, and all the addresses and debates that followed, as I knew well that it was all falsehood, and it distressed me the more, because I saw the deep impression that was made on many of my brethren. I left the house with the firm resolution that on the following Sabbath I would convince the missionary and his associates that Jesus was not the Messiah. I studied the whole following week in the Bible, which I know well, and prepared very important questions to bring before the missionary. This I did Sabbath after Sabbath, with all my energy, but it was the means of bringing me to the *firm conviction* (for which I thank also Mr Warszawiak, whom I now love more than I do my father, mother, wife and children) that I was all that time fighting against God and His truth. May the Lord and Saviour accept of me, and of my family, and grant us true faith." The man who spoke these words is called Abraham E——, and is a well-to-do Jew. He was followed, amid tears and sobs, by Mr Jacob See. "Ah, my Lord, what witness can I bear to Thee? Thou art indeed all in all! Thou hast brought salvation to my desolate heart. I love Thee, but Thou hast loved me much more. Thy blood is my forgiveness. O Thou good Lord!" I must tell you that dear Jacob has, thanks to God, now obtained an excellent situation. Hitherto I was obliged to help him for everything. May the Lord, who knows all the needs of this work, grant His blessing abundantly, and may He stir up His people to support this work. Amen. What our work principally needs is, that we should be able to establish a house in which the poor could get food and a bed, and if possible there should be a little factory—bookbinding or tailoring.

Thus early Mr Warszawiak began to feel the need of a Home, and, thanks be to God, after much patience and earnest effort, a Home for Persecuted Jews was opened January 16, 1892, through the liberality of Scotch and English friends.

Another interesting and hopeful meeting is described in the following letter:—

August 2.—The meeting to-day was in the church, which

was almost as full as it could hold. The Jews throughout showed only love and friendly feeling. The most wonderful circumstance of the day was the case of a dear old Jew who attended our meeting for the first time, and is seventy-two years old. He said to those present, "I praise God who has so unexpectedly brought me here. Oh, if this were true! Can there be a Saviour for me? How then may I not rejoice in my old age. The dear young man has preached so beautifully, that I can say truly I never heard the like in all my life." Then the dear old Jew ran to me and took hold of both my hands with great warmth, "Ach, Herr Redner, I thank you from the bottom of my heart for your sermon." Dear friend, I cannot describe to you what a meeting this was, but the Lord can do great things, can He not?

August 30, 1890.—It is 9 P.M. I am very tired, have other things to do, and much work to prepare for next week, yet I must give you an account of to-day's meeting. Thanks be to God, there was a large attendance of Jews to-day; also, the sermon was specially interesting. At 1 P.M. all the seats round the big table were crowded; at 2 P.M. there were over one hundred Jews present; and at 3 P.M., when I began the sermon, the church was full. I had announced on the former Sabbath that I would preach a specially interesting sermon to-day on the theme, "The Messiah, son of Joseph, and the Messiah, son of David." The Jews believe in two Messiahs, Messiah ben Josef and Messiah ben David. I succeeded, by the help of the

Lord, in convincing my hearers that this is only a Rabbinical doctrine, and not the truth. After this, the debate began, and although only twelve questions were proposed, they were all of great interest, and the Jews present waited breathlessly for my answers to each question. Some one called out, "What salary do you get, Mr Missionary?" I said, "That is not your affair." "No, it is not my affair," answered he, "but I can assure you that though I am only an ordinary working man, I would not undertake your work for 200 dollars a week." When the twelve questions were all answered it was 5.20 P.M., and the meeting was closed. Be it remarked that ticket No. 9, instead of proposing a question, read the following words: "Dear Brethren,—You all ask questions, and since I came here I have not yet found that any one has asked a question which the missionary has not answered out of the Bible. I must say, I fear, it is indeed true that Jesus was the Messiah. I have nothing more to say, Mr Missionary." Pastor Leonhard said one day to his German congregation, "I do not know how it is that the Jews can sit four, five or six hours in a meeting on Saturday, and we cannot get them away till the janitor comes in and says, 'Kinder, nach Hause' (children, go home); and we can hardly get the Christians to sit still one hour." I have had twenty banners with texts in Hebrew prepared for the church, and also in golden Hebrew characters the Lord's Prayer, and the gospel in Isaiah liii. This cost a good deal, but for my work is well worth it.

Sept. 29, 1890.—As I have written enough about other matters to-day, I will only tell you about the holy work that the dear Lord has entrusted to me. Is it not overpowering to see Him carry on the work so wonderfully by the power of the Holy Spirit ? I told you that I expected a large meeting last Saturday, yet I never expected such numbers as actually assembled. The church was as full as it could hold of Jews only. It was a moving sight for me and the Rev. Mr Leonhard to look upon; and I was obliged to go into the next room, and bow my knees before the Lord, that He might richly bestow His blessing. I first read the 6th chap. of the gospel of Matthew, and when we came to the 9th verse, we all prayed the Lord's Prayer together. Then John x. 1-19 was read, and before the sermon Ezek. xxxiv. 1-25. The two chapters are bound together through verses 11-12 and 15-16.

Thank God, I must confess that the Holy Spirit of the Lord helped me greatly, and that the Jews seem to have got quite a new understanding of the truth of the New Covenant. We could see this in the great attention, and also in the fact that not a single one left in the middle of the sermon. We also perceived the effect when the discussion came on. All had joyful countenances, except one man, who has before sought to disturb us, who was deeply concerned, and stood up and said, "Since I came here I am quite broken down, and truly do not know which is best, to be a Jew or a Christian. I would like to believe in salvation through Jesus Christ, and yet to remain a Jew and die a Jew." Afterwards several young men expressed the same thing. I turned the occasion to the best account (too long to relate), and gave myself as an example. Thanks be to the faithful Lord, His Holy Spirit is in our midst, and soon the fruit of the work will appear. Last week I composed a hymn in Jargon, and it was sung at our meeting for the first time. I could compose and print many others, but I fear the expense.

On the first anniversary of his baptism, Mr Warszawiak wrote as follows :—

With "Oh, I thank and praise Thee, my dearest, most gracious Lord and Saviour, for Thy preservation of Thy poor servant during a whole year!" I sprang this morning out of bed soon after 4 A.M., and under a deep sense of the great mercy of deliverance from sin through Jesus, cast myself down before the Lord and cried, "Lord, Lord, preserve me unto the great day of Thy glory!" O wonderful day the 6th October! No other day is to be compared to this chosen day of the grace of God! O what a miracle the mighty God has worked in His weak servant! How can I praise Him enough? I spent the first half of the day very quietly in meditation, considering all the past—the future, and my appearing before His face and He will count me among His sheep, yea, He has already confessed my name before His Father and the angels. O how I rejoice that such a sinful worm as I, am safe in the arms of Jesus.

The first baptism in the De Witt Memorial Church

took place November 16, 1890. Many of Mr Warszawiak's hearers had urgently begged for baptism long before this; they had received regular private instruction, but the pastors of the City Mission were so anxious to test the converts to the utmost, that they were very slow to admit candidates to the fellowship of the church, and rather allowed the converts to get baptism in other churches, or in other towns, and this course was followed by several; but at last a baptism took place, and is described in the following letter :—

Nov. 17, 1890.—Last Saturday's meeting was good, though not so full as usual, but on the Lord's day we had a blessed time. The true sincere brother Jacob See (who was long ago baptized by the Holy Spirit) received the holy ordinance of our Lord's appointment. Dr Schauffler preached, and the Rev. Mr Elsing administered baptism. I could give many particulars, but will only mention one. *All* the Jews who were present at the baptism went up afterwards to See, and instead of hating, cursing, and abusing the neophyte (Taufling), as is customary with Jews, *congratulated* him one by one, shook hands with him in a friendly way, and said, "*May God keep you steadfast in faith.*" The Jews all know what a true man he is, and in fact they envy him. . . . I hope that brothers G—— G—— B—— and J—— are really as true as brother See, and will soon also be united to the Lord. There are many more who ask for baptism, only we fear that they do not seek "Jesus only."

At the close of the year, Mr Warszawiak thus sums up the work accomplished in New York:—

Decr. 31, 1890.—I thank the Lord, who has enabled me, during the past nine months, to hold 152 meetings with the Children of Israel, at which about 8000 Jews have heard the Gospel. I thank Him, that He has helped me to come off victorious in 46 public discussions, and to convince the crowd that Jesus of Nazareth is indeed the true Messiah, that He has also enabled me to distribute 25,000 tracts, and about 1000 Testaments among true Israelites, and that He has permitted me during this short time to visit an immense number of Jewish families, and to proclaim to them the salvation of God. I have distributed, with my own hand, about 120,000 invitation cards among my brethren after the flesh in New York city; 24 of these have become believers in Christ Jesus, and some of them are already baptized. Not a day has passed in which I have not laboured for my dear Saviour, and now I close the year 1890 with great joy and thankfulness and praise to His Holy Name, who has so richly blessed poor me, and preserved me from all evil; above all, I thank Him that He has delivered me from the death of sin by His blood; and now I say with Paul, Rom. viii. 35-39. I don't forget to thank Him that He has made me to be so beloved by my Jewish brethren. Is it not wonderful? I have not received a single

Christmas present from any Christian, but my Jews have all, according to their ability, remembered me, and on Thursday evening they *surprised* me with a present and a hearty congratulation, and sang a specially prepared hymn. For all this, I shall praise my Jesus to all eternity (1 Tim. i. 16, 17). Amen.

Such hard and incessant labour would have been enough to break down the health even of a strong man, and the wonder is that one so fragile could hold out through summer heat and winter cold. About New Year time he caught cold, and once and again lost his voice, and was necessitated to abstain from preaching. He was laid aside for ten days in January, and in March for three weeks, and then had hardly recovered and preached again with wonted vigour, when he was completely prostrated by "La Grippe." His friend and correspondent in Scotland invited him to cross the Atlantic and pay her a visit, and the Committee of the New York City Mission granted him a two months' holiday with continuance of salary, and with a thankful heart he found himself once more in Edinburgh, June 4, 1891, to enjoy much-needed and well-earned rest.

It may not be necessary to illustrate the work of the spring months of 1891 by copious extracts from the letters, but the following, which describe the baptism of a whole family, and the hardships and sufferings to which those who profess their faith in Christ are exposed, cannot be omitted:—

New York, Feb. 3, 1891.—The dear Lord whom you and all the world call Jesus, for He shall save His people from their sins, helps us very, very wonderfully in the work. Not fewer than 1931 Jews visited our mission during the month of January. Many, many have become very earnest latterly. Daily, Jewish brethren beg for baptism, but I put them off as long as we have no arrangement or "Home" in which to protect brethren who are cast out by the Jews. Yet many cannot wait, and run to different churches in the town where they get baptized. And last Sunday, Feb. 1, two of my most earnest catechumens were baptised by Mr Freshman. You know them by name. . . . Yet it is a great joy that they are converted,—be it as it may,—one Lord, one faith, one baptism. In many respects it would be better if these converts could remain with me, but at present I cannot lead forward to baptism any penniless Jew, whom I have no prospect of being able to help afterwards. Yet we do hope to have a baptism in the De Witt Church next Sunday. This dear man is not poor, and has never asked the least help. His name is Reuben Müller, thirty-one years of age, married, and has two children. His dear wife is quite of one mind with him, and wishes also to confess the Saviour, but at present is in the hospital with her children.

Feb. 10.—The baptism of R. M. took place last Sunday morning. I gave a short address, then Mr Elsing questioned him concerning his faith, and then baptized him in the name of the Father, the Son, and the Holy Ghost. May he also have been baptized by the Lord Jesus and His Spirit with the heavenly baptism! Amen. I must say, if all my work had led only to the saving of *this one soul*, I would be satisfied, for brother M. is a very noble man, and a thoroughly true Christian. I praised God with all my heart, when the Jews who were present, at the close of the service, congratulated brother M. Every one shook hands with him, saying, "May God keep you in the religion you have just confessed for ever and ever; but show always your love and true sympathy with your forsaken Jewish brethren, as Mr W. does," etc. Ah, how wonderful! (Isa. xi. 4). But what above all is to be admired is, that his dear wife (an orthodox Rabbinical woman) was so happy when I visited her yesterday in the hospital with Mr M. She kissed her husband and said, "Praise God, praise God! Ah, how changed thou art, as if new-born!" She hopes soon to be able to leave the hospital, and at once be baptized with her two little sons. Ah, Lord Jesus, take this converted family under Thy protection! Amen.

Feb. 24.—You will rejoice when I tell you that the wife and children of our brother M. were baptized the day before yesterday (Sunday) in the De Witt Memorial Church. It was a glorious Lord's Day. First, the baptism took place, then the Lord's Supper was dispensed, and then Mr and Mrs Müller were received as members of the congregation. I hope this act will cause you to praise and bless the dear Saviour Jesus very much, for the love and compassion He has shown to this whole family in delivering them from the death of sin by His precious blood. Many interesting particulars might be related, but my pen is too weak, only I will tell you one thing: One day, Rev. Mr Leonhard said to brother M., "Do you know something of Christian theology?" "Yes," he answered, "I know the best theology—that Christ Jesus died for me." It was in the meeting, and made a great impression on the Jews who were present.

Persecution and suffering soon came to test the faith of the newly-baptized. On the 10th March, Mr Warszawiak, writing from his sick-room, to which he was confined by sore throat and complete loss of voice, writes as follows:—

Mrs M. is very ill, and has been removed to the Belview Hospital, but thank God, she says, "I am ready, I am ready, for He has done all. It is finished." Her brother persecutes her because she has found Jesus, and has succeeded in turning Mr M. out of his situation, and he now suffers for Christ's sake. I must help him with his rent, though, of course, my own sickness gives me extra expenses.

In a letter, dated 14th April, other baptisms are recorded. He writes:—

In the now quiet heart of the poor missionary Hermann, there shone, last Sunday, a bright light. Pure joy and much praise and thanks filled my heart. Early in the morning, the dear Lord Jesus appointed to meet me at His holy table, and in truth I never was so near to Him who died for me as in that hour. My thoughts were all centred on Him, and I remembered all who are dear to me. In the afternoon I had an interview with two great Rabbis of our city, Rabbi Silverman of Temple Immanuel, and Rabbi Schönfeld of Brooklyn, and I had a good opportunity of proclaiming my Lord's name, and was invited by Rabbi S. to a religious discussion in his own house. But, best of all, was the evening service, when two of my Jewish brethren and scholars received holy baptism. One of them you know by name, Mr Bernstein. I have instructed him for a whole year, and he is full of the Spirit. He and his dear wife and three children are now given over to the Lord Jesus Christ, and may He richly bless them! The second, Mr W., I have not been so long acquainted with, but he was brought to a knowledge of the truth of the Gospel ten or twelve years ago, by means of a dear Scotch Christian lady in Constantinople. He is forty-two years old, and looks to Jesus alone for the forgiveness of his sins.

April 21.—The Lord tries Brother M. with many sorrows,

and took from him yesterday his youngest son, but he says with Job (Job i. 24). Do pray for him.

The voyage across the Atlantic did wonders in restoring the energies of the exhausted missionary, and after resting a week with Miss Douglas in her own house, at the same time enjoying fellowship with Dr J. H. Wilson, Mrs Wilson, Rev. J. G. Cunningham, Principal Brown of Aberdeen, and other revered fathers and brethren too numerous to be named, and then in the company of his best friend spending a few lovely summer days in the woods and hills around Aberfeldy, the pressure on his spirit to help the suffering brethren he had left behind in New York became insupportable; he could no longer enjoy his own ease, but must be up and doing, must call forth the sympathy and prayers of Scottish Christians, and tell them how wide a door the Lord had opened for Israel in the United States of America. Accordingly he gladly availed himself of the invitation of the Rev. J. Macrae, Free Church Minister of Aberfeldy, to preach on Sabbath evening, and, despite the obstacle of the English language, thrilled the hearts of the audience, testifying that God is able to graft Israel in again, nay, that He is doing it. So deep was the impression made that, though nothing was said of the pecuniary needs of the mission, spontaneous offerings, accompanied by assurances of prayer, flowed in that night and the following days, after the missionary had left the place; many of the gifts being of the most touching nature, true "widows' mites." The ground being thus broken, invitations came from other places to address meetings. In this way Mr Warszawiak visited Burntisland, Elie, Anstruther, and Glasgow, where he was the guest of that lover of Israel, the Rev. Andrew Bonar, D.D., returning again to Edinburgh, where he gave several addresses, and stirred many hearts to their depths. A paper was drawn up, giving in figures a view of the greatness of the work among the Jews in New York, and naming as the most urgent necessity that a Home should be established for the affording of temporary protection of, and giving employment to, converts and inquirers who are cast out and bitterly persecuted by the Jews. This paper was widely distributed, but the living voice of the messenger was always employed rather in dispelling faint-heartedness as to the hopefulness of Jewish missions and in crying aloud, "God *is* fulfilling His word! God *is* working among His Israel! O come to the help of the Lord!" It was a wonderful joy to the Scotch friends who had seen the young six months'-old convert trembling before his persecutors, who sought to rob him of his Saviour and his faith, as he went out from their sheltering love, come back to them the strong joyful servant of the Lord, who no longer feared the face of man, and who, the Lord being with him, had done valiantly, and won many crowns to put on his Redeemer's head.

This joy was more than shared by the spiritual father of the "Little Prophet," the Rev. Daniel Edward, who, in the good providence of God, visited his native land at this very time. It was considered advisable before returning to New York that Mr W. should visit London, though the friend and brother (Rev. Dr Adolph Saphir) who had the deepest interest in him and in his work, and would have welcomed him and guided all his steps in the great city, had been called away, leaving a sad blank for the young brother. Mr Warszawiak, however, spent nearly three weeks in London, visited as many of the Jewish missions as he could find access to, and had opportunity of preaching Christ to his dear Jewish brethren in Sion Chapel and in Rev. J. Wilkinson's Medical Mission. Through the kind exertions of Miss de Broen of Paris, he had an opportunity of telling the tale of the New York work in Horbury Rooms, and before sailing again for New York, he addressed a large meeting in the Conference Hall, Mildmay, Room 6, convened by the Hebrew Christian Association. He met with much cordial kindness and sympathy from Colonel and Mrs Morton, Mr Samuel Wilkinson, and many other members of that centre of active love for Israel, and received important help for his work from Rev. John Wilkinson, who gave him a grant of twenty thousand New Testaments in Hebrew and Judeo-German portions, and a sum of money to be spent on the distribution.

Followed by the prayers of many new-made friends both in England and Scotland, and carrying with him their bounty for the poor Jewish saints in New York, Mr Warszawiak sailed again on his return voyage from Liverpool on the 22d July. There was reason to fear that a two months' absence might have greatly marred the work, as all the meetings were unavoidably closed during that time. The two pastors of the De Witt Memorial Church had, from the outset, taken the deepest interest in the Jewish work, attended the meetings and strengthened the hands of the missionary, but no one save himself could secure the attention of a Jewish audience, or reach their minds and hearts, so it was inevitable that for a time the work should entirely cease. But how wonderfully all fears were disappointed, and how the work afterwards grew and deepened, will best appear from the following letters. He landed for the second time at New York on the 30th July 1891, and wrote:—

I am safely arrived, after a perfectly delightful voyage. Many Jewish brethren came to meet me.

Aug. 7.—Though it is Friday evening, and I am quite worn out, after a long day's work in the mission, I must explain to you the present position of our Jewish Mission. Since my return, I am more than ever convinced of the absolute necessity of a "Home," not merely in order to teach poor Jews a trade, or to provide a refuge for persecuted ones. If that were all, I would have waited patiently, but, dear friend, the case is this. Hundreds of Jews come about me, and I have no place in which to receive them. During the ten days since my return not fewer than forty-four Jews have come to my house asking baptism, and twenty-three have applied by letter, saying they are convinced that Jesus is the true Messiah, and they want to follow him. A great awakening has taken place among the Jews. The Holy Spirit of God has taken the work among the children of Israel into His own hand, and has worked much more during my absence than when I was here, and that explains how it is that so many now run after me. Every evening the meeting is crowded with Jewish brethren, and yesterday, when I came home, I found thirteen men standing at my door, each wanting a private interview. Naturally, my landlady objects, and says if this is to go on, she cannot, much as she would regret it, let me remain in her house, and says, "Why do you not hire an office?" . . . I am seriously alarmed lest, with so much running about, my strength will again soon give way.

Aug. 25.—My door is constantly beset by Jewish visitors, and the meetings are crowded. Last Saturday we had to open the doors of the adjoining halls, and certainly, at this rate, in a few months, the De Witt Church will be too small for the congregations. I need hardly say that one labourer is quite insufficient. But to whom shall I speak? The dear Christians do not listen to me. Ah, Lord, help, help! Many have recently been converted to the Lord Jesus, and it is impossible for me to tell you about each one; but there is a Miss C——, the daughter of a rich merchant of our city, who has been wonderfully converted. "My heart is moved by a Divine Spirit to believe in Jesus as my only Saviour," was her answer when I asked her why she came to the inquiry-room. I cannot write how this daughter of Israel was praying. I never heard such a prayer in my life, and we here all agree that the dear girl is touched most powerfully by the Holy Spirit of Christ. I ask your special interest in prayer for her. She said she would never be able to leave her parents, as they love her so very much, and are strict Jews; but also she is confessing that she feels "the love of Jesus" more, and much more than that of her dear father and mother. I am earnestly praying for her, believing that she could be a great testimony for the truth of Christ. Amen. Since you have observed the hour of prayer on Saturday, there has been much more blessing on the work. Here also our forty-eight missionaries have resolved to offer special prayer for Israel every Saturday evening.

Sept. 16.—The crowd of hearers was immense last Saturday. It was a touching sight—hundreds of Jews standing to see, waiting to hear the gospel message. I read to them (after a short, warm prayer) the 10th chapter of Hebrews, making all needful explanations; then from the prophet Jeremiah xxxi. 31-34, and took for my text Prov. xxvii. 27. I cannot undertake to repeat the sermon, but only say that many of the hearers were much moved and quickened by the Holy Spirit of God. The demand for different books and tracts which they took away was great—New Testaments, Pilgrim's Progress, Old Paths, etc. Others called out, "Oh, give us the book of this religion!" What pen can describe how the Redeemer of Israel is working here?

Sept. 22.—I am sorry to say that last Saturday there was quite an uproar. Too many people had forced their way into the church, and at 2.45 P.M., when the meeting was opened, the police closed the entrance doors. We who were within proceeded quietly, unconscious of the great commotion in the street. In a short time about 300 Jews gathered at the doors and struggled with the police for admission, showed their invitation cards, offered entrance money, etc., and would on no account move off. At the conclusion of the first meeting, I was obliged to admit the people who had been standing in the street, and preach over again the same sermon on Heb. viii., with Jer. xxxi. 31-34. At the close my strength was quite exhausted. Oh, it was a heavy day's work, but God worked with me by His Holy Spirit. Many earnest Jewish men (there were also about 50 women present) gave their hearts to the beloved Jesus, and now He Himself works among them. What is to happen next? is the question, but dear Dr Schauffler, who was present, and also spoke a few words, promised that he would take steps to provide more room, which announcement was received with jubilant "Bravo" and clapping of hands. O mother, we do not know what the Lord purposes to do, but surely it is a sign of the time when "All Israel shall be saved," and let us praise Him without ceasing. Many Jews impatiently demanded holy baptism, but I am still resolved to wait till the Home is opened, and I can a little shield them from persecution. Two young men were baptized yesterday in other churches.

Sept. 29.—Since last Friday I have said continually, "Bless the Lord, O my soul, and forget not," etc., and oh, that Christ may receive my poor offering, for I have offered my tongue to Him wholly, and my heart is, I believe, already His; the same is with all I possess, even my sins are His; the only desire I have is to lie under Jesu's feet to keep and receive the grace, or any off-fallings from His sweet hands to forlorn sinners. Indeed, the blessed Lord has lately left a fire in my heart that hell cannot cast water on, and I cry and cry again, "Bless the Lord, O my soul," etc. Last Friday evening there were a number of Jews in our meeting who professed faith in Jesus Christ as their personal Redeemer and Saviour. The following day (Saturday) the crowd was larger than ever. . . . Dear Dr Hall, who was present for the first time, was so astonished, that he expressed it in the short address he made to the assembled Jewish brethren. He said, "Looking at this great audience of Jews in the church of Christ Jesus, our beloved Saviour, makes me surely believe that the day of Israel's redemption by Him is very near, if not at hand." Dr Schauffler sent me to preach in behalf of the Jewish Mission in the large church in Haarlem, N.Y., and in the evening I preached in the M'Auly Mission, and, I hope, awakened the interest of many.

Oct. 13, 1891.—The dear Lord Jesus still increases our work, and it seems as if we must cry out, "Hold, Lord, it is enough!" for though the church, the large Sunday schoolroom, and the two class-rooms adjoining are all open (and can contain nearly a thousand people), we are still obliged to send many away every Saturday. We hang up a notice on the front door when the place is full, "Alles besetzt," and on the invitation cards, it is added, No admission after 3 o'clock. On the two last Saturdays—"the Jewish New Year," and the day before the Great Day of Atonement—I preached "Jesus only, and Him crucified," in fact, the contents of both sermons was nothing further than:—

> "Jesus, Jesus, ganz allein
> Macht uns von den Sunden rein,"

and I thank and praise the dear Saviour that He worked so powerfully by his Holy Spirit, that a great multitude of men and women were touched in their hearts and received the truth. Yesterday was the Jewish Day of Atonement, and I had a special meeting at 10 A.M. There were not many Jews present, but it was glorious to hear so many children of Israel pray to Jesus, and ask forgiveness of their sins. Many burst into tears, and cast themselves on Jesus alone, like the Prodigal Son when he returned to his father. We passed two hours in prayer, then I gave a short address and closed the meeting. We then went to Old John Street noon meeting, and then separated and went to the different Jewish Synagogues and distributed many tracts, gospels, and testaments. May the pitiful Lord Jesus finish the work till all Israel is saved!

I cannot describe how it was with me on my "second anniversary" [of his baptism], but, thank God, I was able to see Jesus in all His goodness unto me in the two years past, and, like the disciple whom He loved (I hope He loveth me too), I said, "It is the Lord," and I cried, "My God, my Lord, my Saviour, my Prince, my Redeemer, my Peace, my Life, my Rest, my Rock, my Food, my Shield, my Beauty, my Light."

It is all through Jesus and through His precious blood that I am right, and so I have cast myself for the future on Him only, who asked me very often, "Lovest thou Me *more* than thou didst before?" and I am ashamed to say I feel myself a great debtor in love to Jesus till now, but am trying to pay Him all the debt. Pray for me. . . . I am sorry to be obliged to say that the parents of Miss C—— keep her close at home, because she wanted to become a Christian, but we must hope the Lord will help.

Oct. 20.—Excuse; only a few lines are possible for me. The post closes at twelve midnight. I have but fifteen minutes, and am very ready for bed. The work is enormous, and ten missionaries would find enough to do; but Lord, Lord, Thou knowest how ready I am to do Thy will, and do not murmur in the least!

To-morrow our Committee is to come together and examine several Jewish brethren who insist on being baptized with us. [Here he names eight men and two wives.] I hope and believe that the half, at any rate, will receive holy baptism in our church next Sunday. My oldest scholar, viz., dear old Mr Hermann Alexander, who is seventy-six years of age, was baptized last Saturday. It would be a long story to tell about this dear, aged Israelite, but the long and short of it is, "he is won altogether for Christ Jesus," and, therefore, praise be to the dear Lord. I am told the letter-carrier was here to-day with a registered letter for me. I shall probably get it to-morrow morning, and, no doubt, it is from you with enclosed cheque, so I thank you beforehand, and conclude with warm love, and say, Colos. iii. 24, and send you 2 Thess. ii. 16, 17.

Oct. 27.—I can hardly describe the exceeding great joy that I experienced last Sunday. Thanks be to the Lord! He has delivered four more Jewish brethren unto eternal salvation. The four dear brethren are: Mr Joseph Levy, Sigmund Kern, Simon Gutherz and Max Plevy. The two first-named were baptized at 11 A.M. in the English congregation, and the two latter at 4 P.M. by the German pastor. Certainly, my poor heart was never so full of joy as on this Lord's Day, especially when the dear brethren addressed the congregation and explained why they turned to Christ, "the Son of God." No eye remained dry, every heart was moved, and I wept for joy. Many embraced and kissed the dear baptized ones. If you knew what a severe struggle those dear brethren have passed through before they could resolve to forsake father, mother, brother, sister, bride, and property for Jesus' sake, you would praise the Lord much more for their victory. Remember, too, that Gutherz, Plevy and Kern have desired baptism since last year. The four new brethren are indeed *full* of the Holy Ghost, and the multitude of Jews who were present at their baptism were visibly impressed. Pray tell my friends, and the friends of Israel, what wonders the good Lord is doing in our midst—so that their hope for the salvation of Israel may be strengthened.

Nov. 2.—The Committee met last Saturday, and agreed that I should take a house which would be convenient for myself, and in which I can have an office and six rooms for persecuted Jews, and I hope by degrees to get all arranged as I see to be necessary. . . . Spiritually, we stand under the guidance of our dear Lord and Saviour. My four new brethren are clothed with a fiery robe of love to Jesus Christ, our dear Lord. It is really wonderful with what ardour they all speak of Jesus, and so make the deepest impression on all the other Jewish brethren. I cannot make any exception among them, but Gutherz and Levy are specially filled with the Holy Spirit. Levy said to me this morning, "I have had the honour and joy to-day of enduring much suffering and persecution for my dear Lord. My relations fell upon me, and severely beat and abused me. They afterwards met me in the 'City Works Office,' where I went in search of work, and made a frightful noise, got me out into the street, and with difficulty I came off alive; but," said he, "I will not run away from New York, but show them how willing I am to suffer for my Jesus, who suffered even unto death for my sins." It is much the same with Gutherz and Plevy, who must live in their old Jewish quarter and suffer bitterly daily. Ah, if I but had the Home, how rejoiced would they be! but, thank God, the dear Lord preserves them day by day. We praise the Lord without ceasing; 682 Jews attended last Saturday's meeting, and 29 Jewish women and girls. The Holy Spirit works among us, and will surely bring glory to Jesus. Dear Miss C—— has been sent away from New York by her parents, to an aunt in the country, so as to get her away from the mission. But she wrote, "They could not keep me back from Jesus, my dear Saviour, in whom I sincerely believe in the country as in the city. Oh!" she said, "I suffer so much, I wish best Jesus would take me over to Him, for my heart rests in His." I am glad you pray for this dear child—God bless her!

Nov. 9.—There sound all day in my ears the words from Daily Light:—" I, even I, am the Lord, and beside Me there is no (what no?) no Saviour." O dear mother, I rejoice every hour that I am redeemed by Jesus Christ. I am more than happy to be able to say the Lord is with us evermore. The poor mother of Sigmund Kern took the apostacy of her son from Judaism so deeply to heart, that she became sick and died after a few days. Brother Kern was at first quite overcome, but after a while he called aloud, "O, my Jesus, my mother is dead, but Thou livest; ah, give me strength to endure all and to remain Thine, even if it should cost my life! Lord Jesus, be with me!" . . .

Nov. 18.—In great haste. The Lord has wonderfully guided. After we had searched the whole neighbourhood, and failed to find a house suitable for our "Institute," and when I was on the point of taking a house a long way from the church, a householder called on me and offered his house, four blocks from the church. I rejoice the more, as it is a good house, and the other would have cost more, and is smaller. The expenses at the outset will be large, but I am resolved to use the Lord's money in a most plain way, and only for much-needed things, and we trust the good Saviour to send further help.

Dec. 1.—Will any one in Edinburgh or Glasgow help me for Max Plevy? I would like to send him to the Seminary; he has ability, and is full of zeal and spirit. It costs $400 (£80) for the three years' course of study.

I have followed another plan with dear brother Gutherz. I have sent him to Newark, New Jersey, to open a little mission. There are 200,000 inhabitants, of whom 30,000 are Israelites, and nobody does anything to bring the Gospel to them. G. is full of missionary spirit and love to his brethren.

Dec. 21.—Ah, what a delightful Lord's Day we had yesterday in our De Witt Church! At each service a daughter of Israel came forward and professed faith in Jesus as her own Saviour. In the German service it was dear Mrs Micsei who was led by the hand by her dear husband (a former officer of the Austrian Army, who was converted in 1883) to the Sacrament of Baptism. She addressed the congregation before her baptism, broke down in the middle, soon recovered herself, and went on. Her words forced tears from the eyes of all present. She then knelt down, and the Rev. Brother Leonard baptized her in the name of the "Three-One

True God." In the evening, at the English service, Miss Caroline Prince received Holy Baptism from Rev. Brother Elsing, and then Mr and Mrs Millar came forward, leading their eldest boy by the hand (he had been till now with relations). They begged that he might be admitted into the Covenant of Baptism, which the Rev. Elsing agreed to at once, on the faith of the converted parents. Miss Prince has a truly wonderful history; her parents live here in New York, and are very well off. Her father has a large clothier's business in the Eighth Avenue, but the poor girl was troubled by her parents because she became intimate with a Christian family, and accompanied the children to the Sunday School. Her orthodox mother was so dreadfully enraged that she drove the poor child out of the house; she, Caroline, engaged herself next day as servant to Mrs Niemeier (the lady of my boarding-house); only think what a wonderful leading of providence. Naturally I interested myself more or less in this cast-off sheep of the house of Israel, and now the dear Lord Jesus has gained the victory; and though the blinded parents threatened to shoot her, and me also, she says she has no fear, and gave herself over, body and soul, into the hands of Jesus. Miss Prince also made a little address before her baptism, and if I only had time to tell you all, it is full of interest, especially the letter she wrote to her parents before her baptism, but I have no time, and hope to write more quietly from Clifton Springs, where I am to take a little rest at Christmas.

Here for the present our story must end. It is but a little chapter in the great history of "all that Jesus has done and taught *since* the day that He went on high," and is written to the praise of the glory of His great name, and as another instance that "none ever trusted in the Lord and was disappointed of his hope." These things also are written to strengthen the faith of those who wait and hope for that promised receiving of Israel, which is to be life from the dead to all nations. Israel is the everlasting Nation, that cannot lose itself among the peoples. The recent cruel measures which are driving the thousands of Jews, long settled in Russia and Poland, to fly for refuge to the West, excite our rebuke of the oppressor, and our sympathy with the oppressed; but we also see the hand of the Lord, for the same Jews who in Russia were wholly inaccessible to the Gospel, now in their distress, and with all their old ties broken, welcome the good news that their Messiah is indeed come to be their Deliverer. It is true of a vast number, "they know not what they do" in rejecting Jesus Christ, and His prayer is surely offered for such, "Father, forgive them." May this little book call forth from every reader earnest, believing, expectant prayer for Israel, and for the young Israelite whom the Lord has made His messenger of salvation to his brethren.

May much practical sympathy and help also be evoked. These pages show that "The Little Messianic Prophet" is weighed down under the burden of caring for his many followers, and his heart is often well-nigh broken, because he cannot show them, as well as tell them, of *Christian love*—that love which counts nothing too much, which lays down its life for the brethren.

It naturally occurs to friends of Israel in this country, when they hear of this remarkable movement among the Jews in New York, to say, "This is most interesting, and we thank God for it; but pecuniary help cannot be required in a city like New York, which abounds in rich and liberal Christians, who lead the van in missionary enterprise. Alas, it is not the case as yet, that rich congregations and individuals have come to the help of the New York City Mission, which has done its utmost to meet the needs of the large Jewish population which has recently settled around one of its churches; and had it not been that Mr Warszawiak has friends in Scotland, who could not let such an open door for Israel close without intervention, a grand opportunity would have been for ever lost. In the "New York City Mission Monthly" for November 1891, Dr Schauffler writes:—"We have worked in silence during the past eighteen months. Scarcely any one in New York has heard of this wonderful movement, but now the work is becoming too great for us. We need the sympathy, active co-operation, and prayers of Christian people. The young men who forsake all for Christ must receive a welcome among Christian people. It is a pitiable sight to see the door of every Jewish home and workshop shut in the face of a baptized Jew, while no Christian home or Christian shops are open to him. What impression must such a person get of the Christian religion as he walks the streets of our city, lonely, discouraged, and hungry? I believe many a Christian under like circumstances would be driven to despair." That Dr Schauffler's appeal to his fellow-citizens has not yet met with anything approaching to an adequate response, can only be accounted for by the fact, that a vast proportion of American Christians, who give liberally to Missions for the heathen, despair entirely of Jewish Missions, and think their money can be better spent on any other nationality. The facts are these. The word of God fervently preached has stirred to its depths the refugee orthodox Jews of New York. The numbers who are fully convinced that Jesus is the Christ increase week by week. They are pressed in conscience to confess His name, hundreds have applied for baptism; at this moment there are fifty urgent to be admitted into the Christian church, and making a creditable profession of love to the Saviour; but those who have already been baptized suffer to such an extent temporarily, that the Missionary, and his associates in the work, are forced to hold back those who are not men of independent fortune, and the converts are for the most part young men who have still their way to make in the world. Thus the strange spectacle is presented of a mission abundantly owned of God spiritually, but brought to a stand outwardly for want of temporal help. Nothing but the arousing of the consciences of the Christian citizens of New York, to welcome and help the Jewish brethren, can adequately meet the case. But shall not *we* (Christians who believe the sure word of promise to Israel), in whatever quarter of the world we live, be forward to help a little longer? The sum Mr Warszawiak aimed at to found a Home has been obtained. It was opened on the 17th January, and from the first day has been largely used by inquirers, who visit it to the number of thirty or forty between the hours of nine and twelve daily, besides attending a class from four to six P.M. There are also beds where some houseless converts sleep; but there is no means as yet of setting up a trade or trades to employ those who have been cast out of their former occupations, and there are daily demands to send these young men to other cities, or to college, or to start one and another in some business.

Further particulars will be gladly given to any who wish to help, by MISS DOUGLAS, 1 Rosebery Crescent, Edinburgh.

APPENDIX A.

Since April 1890, Mr Warszawiak has held with the Jews of the City of New York—

Chief meetings, at which attendances from (and even more) ,, ,, 500 up to 800,	78
General meetings, ,, ,, 15 ,, 75,	315
Public religious discussions, ,, 25 ,, 100,	93
Calls and visits made by Mr W. in Jewish stores, workshops, and families, . . over	5000
Mr W. received Jewish visitors at his private house, ... over	1000
Visits received from more or less earnest inquirers in the Inquiry Office, . nearly	400
Jewish letters (of all kind of characters) received by Mr W. (see Appendix B.), . over	1500
Religious tracts distributed, in Hebrew, Jargon-German, French, English, Russian, Polish, Hungarian, etc., . . . nearly	100,000
New Testaments, in ditto, given away and sold, ... about	10,000
Bibles, in ditto, given away and sold, exactly	150

Converts by Confession of Faith, several hundreds.

Converts by Baptism, 33, of whom 13 have been baptized at the Mission Church, and the rest in different other churches.

Note.—Since going to press, news has been received of the intended baptism, on February 27th, of twelve men.

APPENDIX B.

In the preceding Statistical Report, Jewish letters received by Mr Warszawiak are referred to. The following letter, translated from the German, is a specimen:—

To Mr Hermann Warszawiak.

NEW YORK, *Jany.* 5, 1892.

DEAR MR MISSIONARY,—I beg you very much to grant, if possible, the following requests:—

> Teach me to know the Living God.
> Teach me to pray to God.
> Teach me to trust in God.
> Teach me to love God.
> Teach me the Holy Scriptures.
> Teach me the right way to Eternal Life.
> Teach me to love my neighbour.
> Teach me the Holy Gospel.
> Teach me to believe in Christ.
> Teach me Christianity.
> Teach me to know Christ.
> Teach me how to pray to Christ.
> Teach me how to pray to the Holy Spirit.
> Teach me *all* that a Christian man should know.

O dear Mr Missionary, you know that, and I believe you will also do that. I will never be able to repay you with silver and gold, but I will for ever and ever be thankful to you. Dear good Sir, I beg you to have pity on a sinner who writes to you, and who is spiritually poor. D. R.

www.ingramcontent.com/pod-product-compliance
Lightning Source LLC
Chambersburg PA
CBHW061511040426
42450CB00008B/1572